CROCHET FOR D

A collection of adorable crochet sweaters for your pets

TABLE OF CONTENTS

01 Introduction

02 Techniques

BASIC SUPPLIES	3
STITCHES	6
ABBREVIATIONS	12
TIPS & TRICKS	13

03 Collection

RIBBY DOG SWEATER	14
BERNAT SUPER CROCHET COAT	19
BERNAT THAT'S BANANAS	26
COZY SWEATER	34
SEA SWEATER	38
BUMBLE BEE SWEATER	42
GRANNY SQUARE SWEATER	49
CABLES DOG COAT	55
CUTIE DOG SWEATER	61
COZY CANINE	68
DAPPER PUP SWEATER	74
DEVIL DOG	81

INTRODUCTION

Welcome to the delightful world of crocheting cozy sweaters for your furry friend! Perhaps you want to create a festive outfit for a holiday party, or maybe you're looking for a practical way to keep your pup warm on chilly walks. Whatever the reason, **"Crochet for Dog: A collection of adorable crochet sweaters for your pets"** is here to guide you on this fun project. Whether you're a crochet pro or a complete beginner, this guide will provide you with all the essentials to get started.

With clear instructions, step-by-step pictures, and handy pointers, we'll break down each step into easy-to-follow sections, ensuring your confidence grows with every stitch. We'll explore a variety of patterns, from quick knits to cable stitch chic, allowing you to personalize your creation and make it truly unique. Imagine the cuteness overload of seeing your pup sporting a sweater you made with love!

So, grab your yarn, find a comfy spot, and let's create an adorable sweater that will have your pup wagging their tail with joy!

TECHNIQUE

BASIC SUPPLIES

CROCHET HOOK

Your Handy Hook: The Heart of Crocheting!

Before we dive into the world of adorable sweaters, let's get familiar with the star player: your crochet hook! Unlike knitting needles, which come in pairs, crocheting uses a single, trusty hook. But don't be fooled by its simplicity - crochet hooks come in a surprising variety of materials, shapes, and sizes, each offering unique advantages and considerations. Let's explore what makes the perfect hook for you!

YARN

Hook & Yarn Essentials: Tools for Pawsome Sweaters!

Before whipping up adorable pup sweaters, let's grab the essentials: your crochet hook and yarn! We'll explore hook options and yarn varieties to find the purrfect (wink!) combo for your canine creation.

YARN/TAPESTRY NEEDLE

Secret Weapon: The Yarn Needle
Don't let loose ends unravel your masterpiece! Grab a yarn needle (darning or tapestry needle) to weave in leftover yarn and sew pieces together. This quick step keeps your pup's sweater looking sharp!

SCISSORS

Snip, Snip: Finishing Touches
After weaving in the yarn, trim the leftover tail with a pair of sharp scissors. Small scissors are ideal for keeping in your project bag for on-the-go crocheting!

TAPE MEASURE

Bonus Buddy: The Tape Measure
Not essential, but super handy! A tape measure helps you ensure your pup's sweater fits perfectly. Use it to measure your project's dimensions and gauge swatch for ultimate accuracy.

STITCH MARKERS

Tiny Trackers: Stitch Markers
For keeping you on track (pun intended!), consider stitch markers. These little tools help mark important stitches – like round beginnings, row ends, or specific increase/decrease points. They come in handy to ensure your pup's sweater follows the pattern perfectly!

STITCHES

Chain (abbreviation: ch)

If you're working in rows, your first row will be a series of chain stitches.

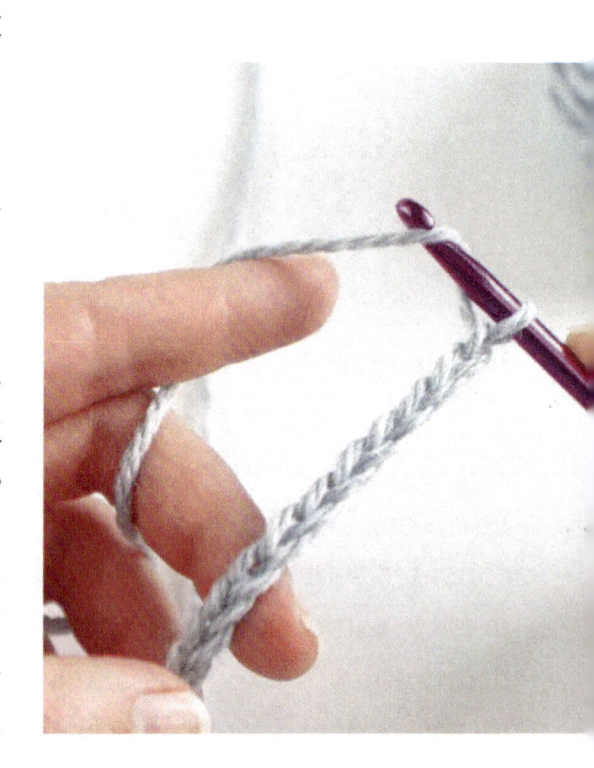

1. With the hook, draw the yarn through the loop.
2. Tighten the loop by pulling it.
3. Wrap the yarn over the hook from back to front. Then pull the hook through the loop already on your hook, carrying the yarn with it.
4. You have now made one chain stitch. Repeat these steps as specified in the pattern to create a foundation chain.

Single Crochet (abbreviation: sc)

Single crochet is the stitch that will be most frequently used in this book.

1. Insert the hook into the next stitch.
2. Wrap the yarn over the hook and pull it through the stitch.
3. Notice there are now two loops on the hook. Wrap the yarn over the hook again and draw it through both loops at once.
4. You have now completed one single crochet.
5. Insert the hook into the next stitch to continue.

Half Double Crochet (abbreviation: hdc)

When starting a new row of half double crochet, work two chain stitches to gain height.

1. Bring your yarn over the hook from back to front before placing the hook in the stitch.
2. Wrap the yarn over the hook and draw the yarn through the stitch. You now have three loops on the hook.
3. Wrap the yarn over the hook again and pull it through all three loops on the hook.
4. You have completed your first half double crochet. To continue, bring your yarn over the hook and insert it in the next stitch.

Double Crochet (abbreviation: dc)

When starting a new row of double crochet, work three chain stitches to gain height. Bring your yarn over the hook from back to front before placing the hook in the stitch.

1. Wrap the yarn over the hook and draw the yarn through the stitch. You now have three loops on the hook.
2. Wrap the yarn over the hook again and pull it through the first two loops on the hook.
3. You now have two loops on the hook. Wrap the yarn over the hook one last time and draw it through both loops on the hook.
4. You have now completed one double crochet. To continue, bring your yarn over the hook and insert it in the next stitch.

Treble Crochet (abbreviation: tr)

The treble crochet stitch includes a front loop, a back loop, a third loop, and a post.

1. With the current loop on the hook, yarn over twice and insert the hook into a stitch.
2. Yarn over again and pull the working yarn through the stitch.
3. You should now have four loops on the crochet hook. Yarn over again and pull the yarn through the first two loops on the hook.
4. Yarn over again and draw the yarn through the next two loops on the hook.
5. Yarn over one last time and draw the yarn through the remaining two loops.

Slip Stitch (abbreviation: sl st)

1. To create a slip stitch into a chain stitch, first make a foundation chain of the desired length. Insert the hook into the last chain of the foundation chain.
2. Yarn over, draw the yarn through the chain and the loop on your hook in one motion to make the slip stitch.
3. To work a slip stitch into row stitches (such as single crochet stitches), insert the hook under the top two loops of the next stitch. Yarn over, draw the yarn through the stitch and the loop on your hook in one motion to complete the slip stitch.

ABBREVIATIONS

- ch(s): chain(s)
- sl st: slip stitch
- sc: single crochet
- dc: double crochet
- tr: treble crochet
- hdc: half double crochet
- dtr: double treble crochet
- st(s): stitch(es)
- rep: repeat
- BLO: back loop only
- FLO: front loop only
- YO: yarn over
- dec: decreas
- inc: increase
- RS: right side
- WS: wrong side
- x - times
- (): repeat instructions between parentheses, as many times as directed
- []: number in brackets at the end of the row/round indicates total number of stitches in a row/round
- *: repeat the instructions following the single asterisk as directed

** : repeat instructions between double asterisks as directed or repeat at specified locations

The patterns are all written using US crochet terms. If you are accustomed to working with UK terms, please note the following differences in stitch names:

US TERM	UK TERM
Single crochet	Double crochet
Half double crochet	Half treble crochet
Double crochet	Treble crochet
Treble crochet	Double treble crochet

TIPS AND TRICKS

1. Gauge Swatch: Start with a small swatch to determine your tension with the yarn and hook you're using.

2. Fix Mistakes Promptly: Address any mistakes promptly to prevent them from affecting the final product.

3. Use Stitch Markers: Mark the beginning and end of rows to maintain straight edges and consistent shaping.

4. Ensure Even Sizing: Maintain consistent tension to prevent the sweater from becoming too tight or loose.

5. Block the Sweater: After finishing, shape the sweater by dampening it slightly and laying it flat to dry. This helps it retain its shape and appearance.

RIBBY DOG SWEATER

Materials:
- 80 g total of Red Heart Super Saver yarn (yarn weight: Medium 4).
- Yarn needle
- Stitch markers or yarn in other color (optional)
- Scissors

Gauge:
14 sts and 13 rows (unstretched) = 4 inches x 4 inches (10 x 10 cm)

Special Stitch:

1. Yarn Over Slip Stitch (yo-slst): Yarn over (yo) and insert the hook into indicated st; yarn over and draw the yarn through.
2. Having the 3 loops on hook, pull/slip the first loop on hook through the next 2 loops on hook to complete a Yarn Over Slip Stitch (yo-slst).
3. Yarn over slip stitch back loops only (yo-slst-blo): work the stitch as described above, but inserting the hook only into the back loops of the stitches
4. dec yo-slst-blo: decrease 2 yo-slsts: yo, insert hook into next st, then insert the hook into the next one, yo and pull through the two sts and the 2 loops on the hook.

Neck Ribbing

Row 1: (RS). 1 yo-slst in 2nd ch from hook and in each ch to end of Chain; ch 1, turn. (6 sts total)

Row 2: 1 yo-slst-bl in each st to end of row, ch 1, turn. (6 sts total)

Rows 3-31: Rep as Row 2; at the end of the last row do not cut yarn and do not fasten off

Body

Row 1 (WS): ch 1 and turn piece to work across the long edge of neck ribbing. Work 1 yo-slst in each row end to end of row.

At the last stitch change to B. Turn. (31 sts total.)

Row 2 (RS): With B ch 1. Work 1 yo-slst-blo in first st, *2 yo-slst-blo in next st, 1 yo-slst-blo in next st. Rep from * to end of row. Turn. (46 sts total)

Row 3 (WS): With B ch 1, Work 1 yo-slst in each st across the row. At the last stitch change to A again. Turn. Continue with A. (46 sts total)

Divide for Leg Openings:

- **Right Front Side:**

Row 1 (WS): ch 1, work yo-slst-blo in each of next 5 sts. Turn. Leave remaining sts unworked.

Rows 2 - 10: ch1, work 1 yo-slst across each of next 5 sts Cut yarn. Fasten off.

• **Back:**
Row 1 (RS): With RS facing, skip next 4 sts of last long row for leg opening.
Join A with slst into back loop of next st, ch1 and work 1 yo-slst-blo same st and 1 yo-slst-blo in each of the next next 27 sts. Turn, leaving the 9 remaining sts of the previous row unworked.
Rows 2 - 10: ch1, work 1 yo-slst-blo in each of the next next 28 sts. Cut yarn. Fasten off.

• **Left Front Side:** With RS facing, skip next 4 sts of last long row for 2nd leg open- Ing.
Join A with slst into back loop of next st, ch1, work 1 yo-slst-blo across last 5 sts.Turn.
Rows 2 - 10: ch1, work 1 yo-slst-blo across each of next 5 sts. Turn. Cut yarn. Fasten off.
Next row: (Join Underbody). Turn piece with RS facing, join yarn A with slst into back loop of 1st st at the beg of right front side, ch1, work 1 yo-slst-blo across first 5 sts. Ch 4 for underarm, work 1 yo-slst-blo in each of the next next 28 sts across the Back, Ch 4 for 2nd. Underarm, work 1 yo-slst across next 5 sts of the other front side. Turn.
Next row (RS): ch1, work 1 yo-slst-blo across first 5 sts, 1 yo-slst in each of next Ch 4; 1 yo-slst-blo in each of the next next 28 sts; 1 yo-slst in each of next Ch 4; work 1 yo-slst-blo across last 5 sts. Turn. (46 sts total)

17

Next row (WS): ch1, work 1 yo-slst-blo in each st (and in each chains at the armholes) across the entire piece. Turn. (46 sts total)

Shape Back (RS) Rows 1-18 : ch 1, cont in yo-slst-blo pattern decreasing 1 st each end of next row (with dec yo-slst-blo), then every other row until you reach to 28 sts in the row (or until you reach a lenght that is 1 inch shorter than the desired finished lenght). Cut yarn. Fasten off.

Ribbed Edging:

Round 1: With RS facing, join A with sl st at the underbody seam. Ch 1. 1 hdc evenly around entire edge, working 2 hdc in corners. Join into round with slst to 1st hdc.

Round 2: Ch 2, work 1 fpdc, 1 bpdc around; in the corners work 2 sts this way: 1dc and 1 fpdc or bpdc (as they come). Join with slst to top of 1st fpdc. Cut yarn. Fasten off.

Ribbing around Leg opening:

Round 1: Join yarn with slst to middle of underarm. Ch 1, work 1 hdc in st around leg opening with 4 decrease sts at the corners; join with slst to top of 1st hdc. (26 sts)

Round 2: ch2, work *1 fpdc, 1 bpdc* around. Cut yarn. Fasten off. Weave in all ends.

BERNAT SUPER CROCHET COAT

Materials:
- Bernat Super Value (5 oz / 140 g)
- Sizes S (M-L-XL)
- Main Color (MC) 1 (1-1-1) ball Contrast A 1 (1-1-1) ball
- Contrast B 1 (1-1-1) ball
- Contrast C 1 (1-1-1) ball
- Contrast D 1 (1-1-1) ball
- Contrast E 1 (1-1-1) ball

Sizes 4 mm (US F) and 4.5 mm (US G) crochet hook or size needed to obtain gauge.

Gaude:
14 dc and 8 rows = 4 ins [10 cm] with larger hook.

Stripe Pattern:
1. Work 1 row each of colors A, B, C, D, E, and MC.
2. Repeat these 6 rows for the stripe pattern throughout the project.

Neck Ribbing:
1. Using the main color (MC) and a smaller hook, chain 8 loosely.
2. 1st row: Single crochet (sc) in the second chain from the hook and in each chain across. Chain 1 and turn.
3. 2nd row: Single crochet in the back loop only of each stitch across. Chain 1 and turn.

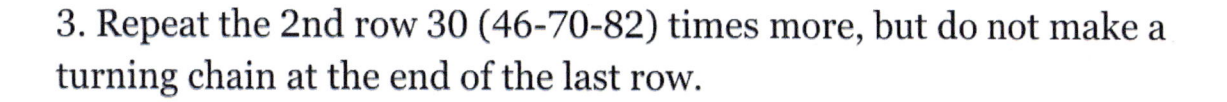

3. Repeat the 2nd row 30 (46-70-82) times more, but do not make a turning chain at the end of the last row.

Body:
1. Switch to a larger hook.
2. 1st row (RS): Chain 3 (counts as first double crochet (dc)). Work 33 (49-73-85) more dc along the long edge of the neck ribbing. 34 (50-74-86) dc total. Join color A, chain 3, and turn.
3. Continue in stripe pattern:
- 2nd row: 1 dc in the first dc (increase made). 1 dc in each dc to the last dc. 2 dc in the last dc (increase made). Chain 3 and turn.
- Repeat the 2nd row 2 (6-10-16) more times. 40 (64-96-120) dc total.

Shape Leg Opening:
First Side:
1. Next row: Skip the first dc. Work 1 dc in each of the next 4 (7-11-15) dc. 5 (8-12-16) dc total. Chain 3 and turn. Leave the remaining stitches unworked.
2. Next row: Skip the first dc. Work 1 dc in the next dc and each dc to the end of the row. Chain 3 and turn.
3. Repeat the last row 1 (3-5-5) more times, omitting the turning chain at the end of the last row. Fasten off.

Center Section:

1. Next row: With the right side (RS) facing, skip the next 4 (7-9-12) dc. Join yarn with a slip stitch in the next dc. Chain 3, then work 1 dc in each of the next 21 (33-53-63) dc. 22 (34-54-64) dc total. Chain 3 and turn. Leave the remaining stitches unworked.
2. Next row: Skip the first dc. Work 1 dc in the next dc and each dc to the end of the row. Chain 3 and turn.
3. Repeat the last row 1 (3-5-5) more times, omitting the turning chain at the end of the last row. Fasten off.

Second Side:

1. Next row: With the RS facing, skip the next 4 (7-9-12) unworked dc. Join yarn with a slip stitch in the next dc. Chain 3, then work 1 dc in each of the next 4 (7-9-12) dc. 5 (8-10-13) dc total. Chain 3 and turn.
2. Next row: Skip the first dc. Work 1 dc in the next dc and each dc to the end of the row. Chain 3 and turn.
3. Repeat the last row 1 (3-5-5) more times.

Joining Row:

1. Skip the first dc. Work 1 dc in the next dc and each dc across the Second Side. Chain 4 (7-9-12) loosely, then work 1 dc in each dc across the Center Section. Chain 4 (7-9-12) loosely, then work 1 dc in each dc across the First Side. Chain 3 and turn.
2. Next row: Skip the first dc. Work 1 dc in each of the next 4 (7-9-12) dc, 1 dc in each of the next 4 (7-9-12) chains, 1 dc in each of the next 22 (34-54-64) dc, 1 dc in each of the next 4 (7-9-12) chains, and 1 dc in each of the next 5 (8-10-13) dc. 40 (64-96-120) dc total. Chain 3 and turn.
3. Next row: Skip the first dc. Work 1 dc in the next dc and each dc across. Chain 3 and turn.
4. Repeat the last row until the work from the Joining Row measures approximately 4½ (7-10½-11½) inches [11.5 (18-26.5-29) cm], ending with the RS facing for the next row and omitting the turning chain at the end of the last row.

Shape Belly:

1. Next row: Slip stitch (ss) in each of the first 7 (10-15-19) dc. Chain 3, then work 1 dc in each of the next 27 (45-67-83) dc. Chain 3 and turn. Leave the remaining stitches unworked. 28 (46-68-84) dc total.
2. Next row: Skip the first dc. Work dc2tog over the next 2 stitches, then work 1 dc in each dc to the last 3 dc. Work dc2tog over the next 2 stitches, then work 1 dc in the last dc. Chain 3 and turn.
3. Repeat the last row 3 (6-9-11) more times. 20 (32-48-60) dc total.

4. Continue working even until the piece from the first row after the neck ribbing measures 10½ (16-22-25) inches [26.5 (40.5-56-63.5) cm], omitting the turning chain at the end of the last row. Fasten off.
5. Sew the seam from the neck ribbing to the belly shaping.

Back Edging:
1. With the RS facing, using MC and the larger hook, join yarn with a slip stitch at the seam. Chain 1.
2. Work 1 row of single crochet (sc) evenly around the belly shaping and back edge, working 3 sc in the corners. Join with a slip stitch to the first sc. Fasten off.

Leg Edging:
1. With the RS facing, using MC and the larger hook, join yarn with a slip stitch in any stitch of the leg opening. Chain 1.
2. Work 1 row of sc evenly around the leg opening. Join with a slip stitch to the first sc. Fasten off.

Leg Bands:
1. With MC, chain 6 loosely.
2. 1st row: Single crochet (sc) in the second chain from the hook and in each chain across. Chain 1 and turn.
3. 2nd row: Working in the back loop only, work 1 sc in each stitch across. Chain 1 and turn.
4. Repeat the 2nd row until the work measures 5 (6-8-9½) inches [12.5 (15-20.5-24) cm] from the beginning. Fasten off.
5. Sew the leg band seam. Sew the leg band to the leg edging.

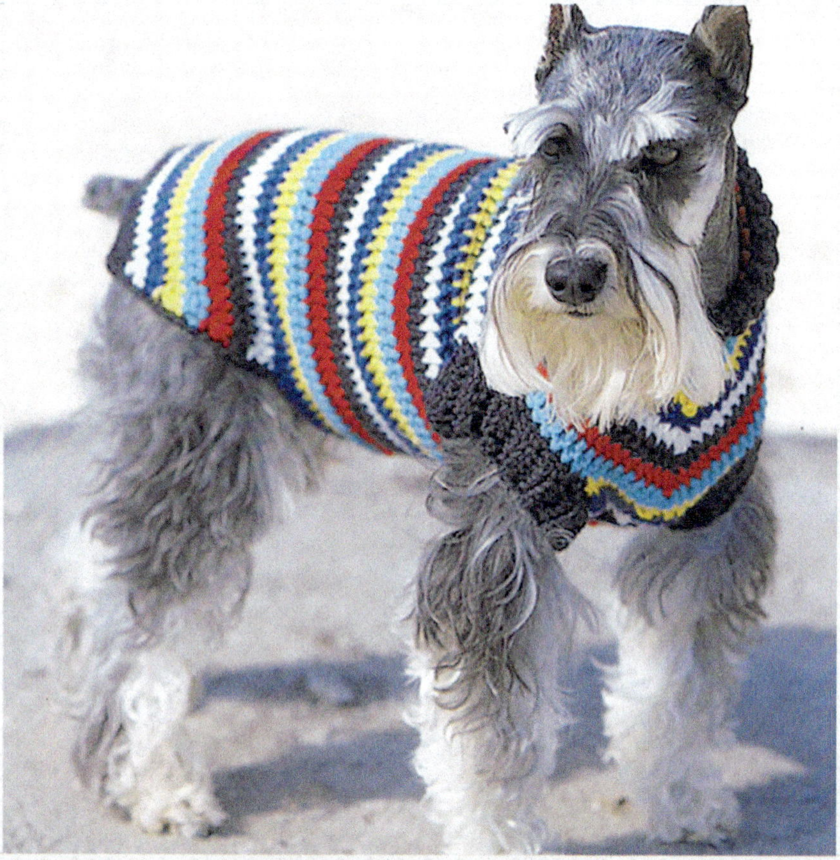

BERNAT THAT'S BANANAS

Materials:
- Bernat® Super Value™ (7 oz/197 g; 440 yds/402 m)
- Contrast A Natural (07414) 1 ball
- Contrast B Chocolate (53013) 1 ball
- Contrast C Baby Pink (07438) 1 ball
- Contrast D Berry (00607) 2 balls
- Contrast E Yellow (07445) 2 balls
- Bernat® Pipsqueak™ (3.5 oz/100 g; 101 yds/92 m)
- Contrast F Whitey White (59005) 1 ball
- Crochet Hooks: U.S. G/6 (4 mm) and U.S. H/8 (5 mm) or size needed to obtain gauge
- 2 stitch markers
- Stuffing
- 4 buttons

Gauge:
13 sc and 14 rows = 4" [10 cm] with larger hook and Bernat® Super Value™ yarn

Size:
This pattern is written for the smallest size

Back:
- Larger hook and yarn D
- Ch 18 (24-30)
- Row 1 (RS): 1 hdc in 3rd ch from hook, 1 hdc in each ch to end, turn (16-28 hdc)
- Row 2: Ch 2, 1 hdc in each hdc to end, turn
- Row 3: Ch 2, 2 hdc in first hdc, 1 hdc in each hdc to last hdc, 2 hdc in last hdc, turn (18-30 hdc)
- Repeat Row 3: 6 (9-11) more times (30-52 hdc)

Body:
- Next 5 rows: Ch 2, 1 hdc in each hdc to end, turn
- Place marker at each end of last row
- Continue working even rows until piece from beginning measures 9 (14-17)" [23 (35.5-43) cm]
- Place marker at each end of last row

Neck Shaping:
- Ch 2, hdc2tog, 1 hdc in each hdc to last 2 hdc, hdc2tog, turn (20-44 sts)
- Repeat last row 4 times more (20-44 sts)
- Fasten off

28

Belly Band:
- Larger hook and yarn D, right side facing
- Join with sl st to left side edge of coat 1½ (2-2½)" [4 (5-6) cm] down from first marked row
- Row 1: Ch 1, work 19 (21-23) sc across to 2nd marked row, turn
- Row 2: Ch 1, 1 sc in each sc to end, turn
- Repeat last row until Belly Band measures 4 (4½-5)" [10 (11.5-12.5) cm]

Buttonhole Row:
- Next row (RS): Ch 1, 1 sc in each of next 1 (2-3) sc, *Ch 3, skip next 3 sc, 1 sc in each of next 4 sc. Rep from * once more. Ch 3, skip next 3 sc, 1 sc in each of last 1 (2-3) sc, turn
- Next row: Ch 1, 1 sc in each sc across, working 3 sc in each ch-3 sp, turn (19-23 sc)
- Next row: Ch 1, 1 sc in each sc across, fasten off
- Sew buttons to correspond to buttonholes on right side edge of Coat

Neckband:
- Larger hook and yarn D, ch 10
- Row 1 (RS): 1 hdc in 3rd ch from hook, 1 hdc in each ch to end, turn (8 hdc)
- Row 2: Ch 2, work 1 hdc in horizontal bar created below st in previous row in each hdc to end, turn
- Repeat last row until Neckband measures approx 8 (12-15)" [20.5 (30.5-38) cm]

Buttonhole in Neckband:
- Next row (RS): Ch 2, 1 hdc in horizontal bar created below st in previous row in each of first 3 hdc, skip next 2 hdc, Ch 2, 1 hdc in horizontal bar created below st in previous row in each of next 3 hdc, turn
- Next row: Ch 1, 1 hdc in horizontal bar created below st in previous row in each of first 3 hdc, 2 hdc in next ch-2 sp, 1 hdc in horizontal bar created below st in previous row in each of next 3 hdc, fasten off
- Sew Neckband to neck edge of Coat

Ice Cream Scoops (make 1 in each yarn A, B, and C):
- Smaller hook, ch 2
- Round 1: 8 sc in 2nd ch from hook, join with sl st to first sc
- Round 2: Ch 1, 2 sc in each sc around, join with sl st to first sc (16 sc)
- Follow instructions for rounds 3-8

Sizes M and L Only - Crochet Coat Instructions
Ice Cream Scoops (Rounds 9-14):
- Round 9 (all sizes): Ch 1, 1 sc in first sc, 1 sc in each of next 2 sc, *2 sc in next sc, 1 sc in each of next 3 sc. Rep from * to last sc, 2 sc in last sc, join with sl st to first sc (40 sc).
- Rounds 10 & 11 (all sizes): Ch 1, 1 sc in each sc around, join with sl st to first sc.

Size L Only:
- Round 12: Ch 1, 1 sc in first sc, 1 sc in each of next 3 sc, *2 sc in next sc, 1 sc in each of next 4 sc. Rep from * to last sc, 2 sc in last sc, join with sl st to first sc (48 sc).
- Rounds 13 & 14 (Size L only): Ch 1, 1 sc in each sc around, join with sl st to first sc.

All Sizes (Rounds 15-20):
- Rounds 15 & 16 (all sizes): Ch 1, 1 sc in each sc around, join with sl st to first sc.
- Round 17 (all sizes): Ch 3 (counts as dc), working in front loops only, 3 dc in first sc, *4 dc in next sc. Rep from * around, join with sl st to top of ch 3, fasten off.

Ice Cream Whip Cream (Make 3):
- Larger hook and yarn F
- Ch 4, join with sl st to form ring.
- Round 1: Ch 4 (counts as tr), 24 tr in ring, join with sl st to top of ch 4, fasten off.

Cherry (Make 3):
- Yarn D and larger hook
- Ch 2
- Round 1: 6 sc in 2nd ch from hook, join with sl st to first sc.
- Round 2: Ch 1, 2 sc in each sc around, join with sl st to first sc (12 sc).
- Rounds 3 & 4 (Cherry): Ch 1, 1 sc in each sc around, join with sl st to first sc.
- Round 5 (Cherry): Ch 1, (sc2tog) 6 times, join with sl st to first st (6 sts). Stuff Cherry. Break yarn, leaving a long end for sewing. Thread end through remaining stitches and draw up tightly. Fasten securely.

Bananas (Make 2):
- Smaller hook and yarn E
- Ch 2
- Round 1 (Banana): 6 sc in 2nd ch from hook, join with sl st to first sc (6 sc).
- Round 2 (Banana): Ch 1, 1 sc in each sc around, join with sl st to first sc.
- Round 3 (Banana): Ch 1, 2 sc in each sc around, join with sl st to first sc (12 sc).
- Rounds 4 & 5 (Banana): Ch 1, 1 sc in each sc around, join with sl st to first sc.

Banana Shaping (Rounds 6-16):
- Round 6 (Banana): Ch 1, 2 sc in first sc, *1 sc in next sc, 2 sc in next sc. Rep from * to last sc, 1 sc in last sc, join with sl st to first sc (18 sc).
- Rounds 7 & 8 (Banana): As Rounds 4 & 5.
- Round 9 (Banana): Ch 1, 2 sc in first sc, *1 sc in each of next 2 sc, 2 sc in next sc. Rep from * to last 2 sc, 1 sc in each of last 2 sc, join with sl st to first sc (24 sc).
- Rounds 10 & 11 (Banana): As Rounds 4 & 5.
- Round 12 (Banana): Ch 1, 2 sc in first sc, *1 sc in each of next 3 sc, 2 sc in next sc. Rep from * to last 3 sc, 1 sc in each of last 3 sc, join with sl st to first sc (30 sc).

Banana Whip Cream:
- With larger hook and F, ch 34.
- 1st row: 1 dc in 4th ch from hook.
- 1 dc in each ch to end of chain. Turn.
- 2nd row: Ch 3 (counts as dc). 1 dc in each dc to end of row. Fasten off.

COZY SWEATER

34

Materials:
- Red Heart® Super Saver® O'Go™ (Prints: 5 oz/141 g; 236 yds/215 m)
- Size U.S. I/9 (5.5 mm) crochet hook or size needed to obtain gauge
- Yarn needle

Gauge:
12 sts and 16 rows = 4" [10 cm] in pat.

Texture Pat

- 1st row: (WS). Ch 1. 1 sc in first sc. *Lsc over next sc. 1 sc in next sc. Rep from * to end of row. Turn.
- 2nd row: Ch 1. 1 sc in each st to end of row. Turn.
- These 2 rows form pat.

NECKBAND

- Ch 6.
- 1st row: (RS). 1 sc in 2nd ch from hook and in each ch to end of chain. Turn. 5 sc.
- 2nd row: Ch 1. 1 scbl in each sc to end of row. Turn.
- Rep 2nd row until 29 (39-49) rows have been worked. Fasten off.

BODY

- 1st row: (RS). Working across long edge of Neckband. Ch 1. 1 sc in each row end to end of row. Turn. 29 (39-49) sc.
- 2nd row: Ch 1. 1 (2-1) sc in first sc. *2 sc in next sc. 1 sc in next sc. Rep from * to end of row 43 (59-73) sc.
- 3rd row: Ch 1. 1 sc in each sc to end of row. Turn.
- Proceed in Texture Pat for 2 rows.

Divide for Leg Openings:

- 1st row: (WS). Keeping cont of pat, pat across first 5 (7-9) sts. Turn. Leave rem sts unworked. Work even in pat on these sts for 9 (13-17) rows more. Fasten off.
- With WS facing, skip next 3 (5-7) sts of last long row for leg opening. Join yarn and pat across next 27 (35-41) sts for Back for 10 (14-18) rows. Fasten off.
- With WS facing, skip next 3 (5-7) sts of last long row for 2nd leg opening. Join yarn and pat across last 5 (7-9) sts for 10 (14-18) rows. Do not fasten off.
- Next row: (Join Underbody). Pat across first 5 (7-9) sts. Ch 3 (5-7). Pat across next 27 (35-41) sts. Ch 3 (5-7). Pat across last 5 (7-9) sts. Turn.
- Next row: Pat across first 5 (7-9) sts. 1 sc in each of next 3 (5-7) ch. Pat across next 27 (35-41) sts. 1 sc in each of next 3 (5-7) ch. Pat across last 5 (7-9) sts. Turn. 43 (59-73) sts. Work 1 row even in pat.

Shape Back: Keeping cont of pat, dec 1 st each end of next row, then every other row 13 times more. 15 (31-45) sts. Fasten off.
Note: Join all rnds with sl st to first st.

Leg Openings:
- 1st rnd: (RS) Join yarn with sl st to any st at leg opening. Ch 1. 1 sc evenly around. Join.
- 2nd rnd: Ch 1. 1 sc in same sp as sl st. *Sc2tog. 1 sc in next st. Rep from * around. Join.
- 3rd rnd: Ch 1. 1 sc in each sc around. Join.
- 4th and 5th rnds: As 2nd and 3rd rnds.
- 6th rnd: Ch 1. Working from left to right, instead of from right to left, as usual, work 1 reverse sc in each sc around. Join. Fasten off.

FINISHING
- Sew underbody seam from Neckband to first shaping row of Back.

Edging:
- With RS facing, join yarn with sl st at seam. Ch 1. 1 sc evenly around entire edge, working 3 sc in corners. Join.
- Next rnd: Ch 1. Working from left to right, instead of from right to left, as usual, work 1 reverse sc in each sc around. Join. Fasten off.

SEA SWEATER

38

Materials:
- Navy (34022): 1, 1, 2, 2 ball(s)
- Size U.S. J/10 (6 mm) crochet hook or size needed to obtain gauge
- Stitch markers

Gauge:
10 sc and 10 rows = 4" (10 cm).

- Ch 26 (32-38-44).
- 1st row: (RS). 1 sc in 2nd ch from hook. 1 sc in each ch to end of ch. Turn. 25 (31-37-43) sts.
- 2nd row: Ch 1. 1 sc in each sc across. Turn.
- Proceed in pat as follows:
- 1st row: (RS). Ch 1. 1 sc in first st. *1 dc in next st. 1 sc in next st. Rep from * to end of row. Turn.
- 2nd row: Ch 3 (counts as dc). *1 sc in next dc. 1 dc in next sc. Rep from * to end of row. Turn.
- 3rd row: Ch 1. 2 sc in first dc (inc made). *1 dc in next sc. 1 sc in next dc. Rep from * to last 2 sts. 1 dc in next sc. 2 sc in last dc (inc made). Turn. 27 (33-39-45) sts.

- 4th row: Ch 3 (counts as dc). 1 dc in first sc (inc made). *1 dc in next sc. 1 sc in next dc. Rep from * to last 2 sts. 1 dc in next sc. 2 dc in last sc (inc made). Turn. 29 (35-41-47) sts.
- 5th row: Ch 1. 2 sc in first dc (inc made). 1 dc in next dc. *1 sc in next dc. 1 dc in next sc. Rep from * to last 3 sts. 1 sc in next dc. 1 dc in next sc. 2 sc in last dc (inc made). Turn. 31 (37-43-49) sts.
- Rep 4th and 5th rows 0 (1-1-2) time(s) more, then 4th row 0 (0-1-1) time(s) more. 31 (41-49-59) sts.
- Work 1 row even in pat.

Leg Openings:
- Next row: (RS). Pat across 2 (3-5-7) sts. Sl st across next 4 (4-4-6) sts. Ch 1. Pat across 19 (27-31-33) sts. Sl st across next 4 (4-4-6) sts. Pat to end of row. Turn.
- Note: All Leg sections are worked at the same time using separate balls of yarn for each section.
- Work 1 (1½-1½-2½)" [2.5 (4-4-6) cm] in pat, ending on a RS row.

Joining row:
- (WS). Pat across 2 (3-5-7) sts. Ch 4 (4-4-6). Pat across 19 (27-31-33) sts. Ch 4 (4-4-6). Pat to end of row. Turn.
- Next row: Pat across 2 (3-5-7) sts. Pat across 4 (4-4-6) ch. Pat across 19 (27-31-33) sts. Pat across 4 (4-4-6) ch. Pat to end of row. Turn. 31 (41-49-59) sts. Cont even in pat until work after neckband measures 5 (6½-8-11)" [12.5 (16.5-20.5-28) cm], ending on a WS row. Place marker at each end of last row.

Back Shaping:

- Next row: Sl st across first 3 (3-5-5) sts. Ch 1. Pat to last 3 (3-5-5) sts. Turn. Leave rem sts unworked. 25 (35-39-49) sts.
- Next row: Ch 1. Draw up a loop in each of first 2 sts. Yoh and draw through all loops on hook - Sc2tog made. Pat to last 2 sts. Sc2tog over last 2 sts. Turn.
- Rep last row 1 (4-5-7) time(s) more. 21 (25-27-33) sts rem.
- Cont even in pat until work after neckband measures 10 (12½-15½-21)" [25.5 (32-39.5-53.5) cm], ending on a WS row. Fasten off.

Back Edging:

- 1st row: (RS). Join yarn with sl st at marker. Ch 1. Work sc evenly across back edge to opposite marker. Turn.
- 2nd row: Ch 1. 1 sc in each sc across. Fasten off. Sew neck and belly seam.

Leg Edging:

- 1st rnd: (RS). Join yarn with sl st at leg opening. Ch 1. Work sc evenly around. Join with sl st to first sc.
- 2nd rnd: Ch 1. 1 sc in each sc around. Join with sl st to first sc. Fasten off.

BUMBLE BEE SWEATER

Materials:
- RED HEART® "Super Saver®" yarn:
- 1 skein each of 0312 Black (CA), 0932 Zebra (CB), and 0320 Cornmeal (CC)
- Crochet Hook: 5.5mm [US I-9]
- Yarn needle
- Two ¾" buttons
- Four 12" black chenille stems

Gauge:
- 12 sts = 4 inches; Rows 1-9 = 4 inches in single crochet. Check your gauge. Use any size hook to obtain the gauge.
- To Fit Chest: 18 (23, 28) inches
- To Fit Neck: 16 (18, 20) inches
- To Fit Length: 10 (12, 16) inches

Note: The "ch 2" at the beginning of double crochet (dc) rows does NOT count as a stitch. Do not work into the "ch 2".

Body:
- With CA, chain 50 (65, 74).
- Row 1 (Right Side): Dc in 3rd chain from hook, * skip next ch, 2 dc in next ch; repeat from * to last 1 (0, 1) ch; dc in last 1 (0, 1) ch; turn – 48 (63, 72) sts.
- Row 2: With CB, ch 1, sc in first 2 dc; * [yo and draw up a loop, yo and draw through 2 loops] twice all in next dc, yo and draw through 3 loops on hook – dc cluster made; sc in next 2 dc; repeat from * to last dc; sc in last dc; turn.
- Row 3: With CC, ch 1, sc in each st across; turn.
- Row 4: With CC, ch 2, dc in first sc, * skip next sc, 2 dc in next sc; repeat from * to last sc; dc in last sc; turn.
- Row 5: With CC, ch 1, sc in each dc across; turn.
- Row 6: With CA, ch 1, sc in each sc across; turn.
- Row 7: With CA, repeat Row 4.
- Row 8: With CB, repeat Row 2.
- Rows 9-18 (9-24, 9-30): Repeat Rows 3-8 one (2, 3) more times, then repeat Rows 3-6 once more. Fasten off.
- Row 19 (25, 31): With right side facing, skip first 6 (9, 12) sc, join CA in next sc; ch 2, dc in same sc, [skip next sc, 2 dc in next sc] 17 (22, 23) times, dc in next 1 (0, 1) sc; turn – 36 (45, 48) dc.
- Row 20 (26, 32): Ch 1, sc in each dc across. Fasten off.

Neckband - Right Side:

- Row 1: With right side facing, join CC in first sc of last long row; ch 1, sc in 8 (10, 10) sc; turn.
- Rows 2-12 (2-12, 2-16): Work in sc, working 3 more rows with CC, then 4 rows CA, then 4 rows CC, then 0 (0, 4) rows CA.
- Buttonhole Row 13 (13, 17): Ch 1, sc in first sc, [ch 2, skip next 2 sc, sc in next 1 (2, 2) sc] twice, sc in last sc; turn.
- Row 14 (14, 18): Ch 1, sc in first sc, [2 sc in space, sc in next 1 (2, 2) sc] twice, sc in last sc. Fasten off.

Neckband - Left Side:
- Row 1: With right side facing, skip center 20 (25, 28) sc of last long row, join CC in next sc; ch 1, sc in last 8 (10, 10) sc; turn.
- Rows 2-12 (2-12, 2-16): Work in sc and work 3 more rows with CC, then 4 rows CA, then 4 rows CC, then 0 (0, 4) rows CA. Fasten off.
- Neck Edging: With right side facing, join CB to Right Neckband; ch 1, sc evenly around entire neck edge. Fasten off.
- Sew buttons to Left Neckband to correspond to buttonholes. Sew body seam.

Wings (Make 2):
- With CC, ch 4; join with a slip stitch to form a ring.
- Round 1: 6 sc in ring; do not join but work in continuous rounds.
- Round 2: 2 sc in each sc around – 12 sc.
- Round 3: [Sc in sc, 2 sc in next sc] 6 times – 18 sc.
- Round 4: [Sc in 2 sc, 2 sc in next sc] 6 times; TURN – 24 sc.
- Shape Bottom of Wing-Row 5: Ch 1, skip first sc, [sc in next 3 sc, 2 sc in next stitch] 4 times, sc in next 3 sc; turn – 23 sc.
- Row 6: Ch 1, skip first sc, sc in each sc to end; turn – 22 sc.
- Row 7: Ch 2, dc in first 4 sc, [2 dc in next sc, dc in next 5 sc] 3 times; turn – 25 sc
- Size Small Only: Turn to work 12 sc evenly across bottom of wing. Fasten off.
- Medium and Large-Row 8: Ch 2, hdc in first 6 dc, 2 hdc in next dc, [hdc in next 2 dc, 2 hdc in next dc] 4 times, hdc in last 6 dc – 30 hdc. Turn to work (14, 14) sc evenly across bottom of wing. Fasten off.

- With wrong sides together, sew the bottoms of the 2 wings together. Weave a chenille stem through the stitches of Row 7 or 8 on each wing. Trim and bend the tips of the chenille stems over at each end to secure in place. Sew the bottom edge of the wings to the center top of the sweater, 1 inch down from the neck edging.

Headband:
- With CC, ch 11.
- Row 1 (Right Side): Sc in 2nd chain from hook, sc in each chain across; turn – 10 sc.
- Row 2: Ch 1, sc in each sc across; turn. (10 sts)
- Rows 3-12 (3-12, 3-16): Repeat Row 2 working 2 more rows with CC, then 4 rows CA, then 4 rows CC, then 0 (0, 4) rows CA. Fasten off.

Headband Ear Flaps - First Half:
- Row 1: With right side facing, join CA to either end of headband; ch 1, sc in first 4 sc; turn.
- Rows 2-10: Ch 1, sc to end; turn. Fasten off at end of Row 10.

Ear Flaps - Second Half:
- Row 1: With right side facing, skip next 2 sc on same end of headband, join CA in next sc; ch 1, sc in last 4 sc; turn.
- Rows 2-10: Ch 1, sc to end; turn.
- Join Flaps-Row 11: Ch 1, sc in next 4 sc, bring First Half around and sc in each of the 4 sc of First Half; turn – 8 sc.
- Row 12: Ch 1, sc to end.
- Row 13: Ch 1, skip first sc, sc in next 5 sc, skip next sc, sc in last sc; turn – 6 sc.
- Row 14: Ch 1, skip first sc, sc in next 3 sc, skip next sc, sc in last sc – 4 sc. Fasten off. Repeat Rows 1-14 on the opposite side of headband.

Antenna Rings (Make 2):
- With CA, ch 2; 6 sc in 2nd chain from hook; join with a slip stitch in first sc. Fasten off.
- Sew antenna rings to the top of the headband. Weave folded chenille stems in each of the antenna rings, twist the chenille stems together, and curl the tips.

Headband Tie (Make 2):
- With CA and CB held together as one, ch 12. Fasten off. Sew to the end of each ear flap.

GRANNY SQUARE SWEATER

Materials:
- RED HEART® "Soft Yarn™":
- 1 (2, 2) Balls No. 4614 Black (CA)
- 1 ball each of:
  - No. 9114 Honey (CB)
  - No. 9779 Berry (CC)
  - No. 9522 Leaf (CD)
  - No. 4422 Tangerine (CE)
  - No. 9518 Teal (CF)
  - No. 9520 Seafoam (CG)
  - No. 4601 Off White (CH)
  - No. 6768 Pink (CI)
  - No. 3729 Grape (CJ)
- Crochet Hook: 5mm [US H-8]
- Yarn needle
- One ¾" button

Gauge:
- Square = 4.5" x 4.5". Check your gauge. Use any size hook to obtain the gauge.

To Fit:
- Chest: 19 (23, 28)"
- Neck: 16 (18, 20)"
- Length: 10 (12, 16)"

Basic Granny Square:
1. Chain 6; join with a slip stitch to form a ring.
2. Round 1: Chain 5 (counts as dc, chain 2), [3 dc in ring, chain 2] 3 times, 2 dc in ring; join with a slip stitch in 3rd chain of chain-5. Fasten off.
3. Round 2: Join yarn in any chain-2 space; chain 5, 3 dc in same space, [chain 1, (3 dc, chain 2, 3 dc) all in next space] 3 times, chain 1, 2 dc in beginning space; join. Fasten off.
4. Round 3: Join yarn in any chain-2 space; chain 5, 3 dc in same space, chain 1, 3 dc in next chain-1 space, chain 1*, (3 dc, chain 2, 3 dc) all in corner chain-2 space; repeat from * around, end at **; 2 dc in beginning space; join. Fasten off.
5. Round 4: Join yarn in any chain-2 space; chain 5, 3 dc in same space, [chain 1, 3 dc in next space] twice, chain 1*, (3 dc, chain 2, 3 dc) all in corner chain-2 space; repeat from * around, end at **; 2 dc in beginning space; join. Fasten off.

Color Sequence for Squares:
- Make 2 (3, 4) squares in the following color sequence:
    - Round 1: CB
    - Round 2: CC
    - Round 3: CD
    - Round 4: CA
- Make 2 (3, 4) squares in the following color sequence:
    - Round 1: CE
    - Round 2: CF
    - Round 3: CG
    - Round 4: CA
- Make 2 (3, 4) squares in the following color sequence:
    - Round 1: CH
    - Round 2: CI
    - Round 3: CJ
    - Round 4: CA

Body:
- Sew 6 (9, 12) squares together. Weave in ends.

Neck:
- Sew one square on each side of the body.
- Make a chain 20 (25, 30)" long and weave in and out of granny squares for neck closure.

Chest Panel - Size Small:
- Make 1 square in colors of your choice.
- Row 5: Join yarn in any corner space; chain 3, 2 dc in same space, [chain 1, 3 dc in chain-1 space] 3 times, chain 1, 3 dc in next corner space. Fasten off. Weave in ends.

Chest Panel - Sizes Medium and Large:
- Make 1 square in colors of your choice.
- Round 5: Join yarn in any chain-2 space; chain 5, 3 dc in same space, [chain 1, 3 dc in next space] 3 times, chain 1**, (3 dc, chain 2, 3 dc) all in next corner space; repeat from * around, end at **; 2 dc in beginning space; join. Fasten off.
- Round 6: Join yarn in any chain-2 space; chain 5, 3 dc in same space, [chain 1, 3 dc in next space] 4 times, chain 1**, (3 dc, chain 2, 3 dc) all in next corner space; repeat from * around, end at **; 2 dc in beginning space; join. Fasten off.
- Row 7: Join yarn in any chain-2 space; chain 3, 2 dc in same space, [chain 1, 3 dc in chain-1 space] 5 times, chain 1, 3 dc in next corner space. Fasten off. Weave in ends.

Finishing:
- Sew the chest panel to both sides of the body.
- Sew on one button at the neck for closure, using a chain-1 space as the buttonhole.
- Weave in ends.

CABLES DOG COAT

Materials:
- Red Heart® Super Saver™ (Flecks: 5 oz/141 g; 260 yds/238 m)
- Sizes: S, M, L, XL
- Aran Fleck (4313): 1 ball (S), 2 balls (M, L, XL)
- Hook: Use a size U.S. H/8 (5 mm) crochet hook or a hook size that ensures the correct gauge. You will also need stitch markers and a yarn needle.

GAUGE
- 13 hdc and 10 rows = 4" [10 cm]

INSTRUCTIONS
- These instructions are for the smallest size. If adjustments for larger sizes are needed, they will be shown in parentheses. Each size's numbers will be consistently shown in the same color throughout the pattern. If a single number is given in black, it applies to all sizes.

Cable Panel (worked over 22 sts)
- 1st row:
- (1 dcfp around next st) twice. 1 hdc in each of next 2 hdc. Skip next 3 sts. (1 trfp around next st) 3 times. Working in front of sts just worked, 1 trfp around each of 3 skipped sts. 1 hdc in each of next 2 hdc. Skip next 3 sts. (1 trfp around next st) 3 times. Working behind sts just worked, 1 trfp around each of 3 skipped sts. 1 hdc in each of next 2 hdc. (1 dcfp around next st) twice.
- 2nd row:
- (1 dcbp around next st) twice. 1 hdc in each of next 2 sts. 1 dcbp around each of next 6 sts. 1 hdc in each of next 2 sts. 1 dcbp around each of next 6 sts. 1 hdc in each of next 2 sts. (1 dcbp around next st) twice.
- 3rd row:
- (1 dcfp around next st) twice. 1 hdc in each of next 2 sts. 1 dcfp around each of next 6 sts. 1 hdc in each of next 2 sts. 1 dcfp around each of next 6 sts. 1 hdc in each of next 2 sts. (1 dcfp around next st) twice.
- 4th row:
- Repeat the 2nd row.
- Repeat 1st to 4th rows to create the Cable Panel pattern. Note: Ch 2 at the beginning of rows does not count as a stitch.

DOG COAT
Collar:
- Ch 11 loosely.
- 1st row: 1 sc in 2nd ch from hook. 1 sc in each ch to end of chain. Turn. 10 sc.
- 2nd row: Ch 1. 1 scbl in each st to end of row. Turn.
- Repeat the 2nd row 34 (44-54-62) times more. Do not break yarn.

Body:
- 1st row: (RS). Ch 1. Work 36 (46-56-64) sc across the long edge of the Collar. Turn. 36 (46-56-64) sc.
- 2nd row: Ch 2. 2 hdc in the first st. 1 hdc in each sc to the last st. 2 hdc in the last st. Turn. 38 (48-58-66) hdc. Place a marker at the end of the row.
- Proceed with the pattern as follows:
- 1st row: (RS). Ch 2. 2 hdc in the first hdc. 1 hdc in each of the next 7 (12-17-21) hdc. Work 1st row of the Cable Panel across the next 22 sts. 1 hdc in each of the next 7 (12-17-21) hdc. 2 hdc in the last hdc. Turn. 40 (50-60-68) sts.
- 2nd row: Ch 2. 2 hdc in the first hdc. 1 hdc in each of the next 8 (13-18-22) hdc. Work 2nd row of the Cable Panel across the next 22 sts. 1 hdc in each of the next 8 (13-18-22) hdc. 2 hdc in the last hdc. Turn. 42 (52-62-70) sts.
- The Cable Panel pattern and side increases are now established.
- Continue in the pattern, working 2 hdc at each end on the next 2 (5-5-7) rows. 46 (62-72-84) sts.
- Work 0 (1-3-3) row(s) even in the pattern.

Leg Openings:

- 1st row: (RS). Ch 1. 1 hdc in each of the first 4 (6-8-10) hdc. Sl st across the next 4 (5-7-9) sts. Ch 2. Pattern across the next 30 (40-42-46) sts. Sl st across the next 4 (5-7-9) sc. Ch 2. 1 hdc in each hdc to the end of the row. Turn.
- Note: All leg sections are worked at the same time using separate balls of yarn for each section.
- Continue in the pattern, working 3 (5-5-9) rows even, ending on a WS row.

Joining Row:

- (RS). Ch 2. 1 hdc in each of the first 4 (6-8-10) hdc. Ch 4 (5-7-9). Pattern across the next 30 (40-42-46) sts. Ch 4 (5-7-9). 1 hdc in each hdc to the end of the row. Turn.
- Next row: Ch 2. 1 hdc in each of the first 4 (6-8-10) hdc. 1 hdc in each of the next 4 (5-7-9) ch. Pattern across the next 30 (40-42-46) sts. 1 hdc in each of the next 4 (5-7-9) ch. 1 hdc in each hdc to the end of the row. Turn. 46 (62-72-84) sts.
- Continue in the pattern, working 2 (4-4-6) rows even, ending on a WS row. Place markers at each end of the last row.

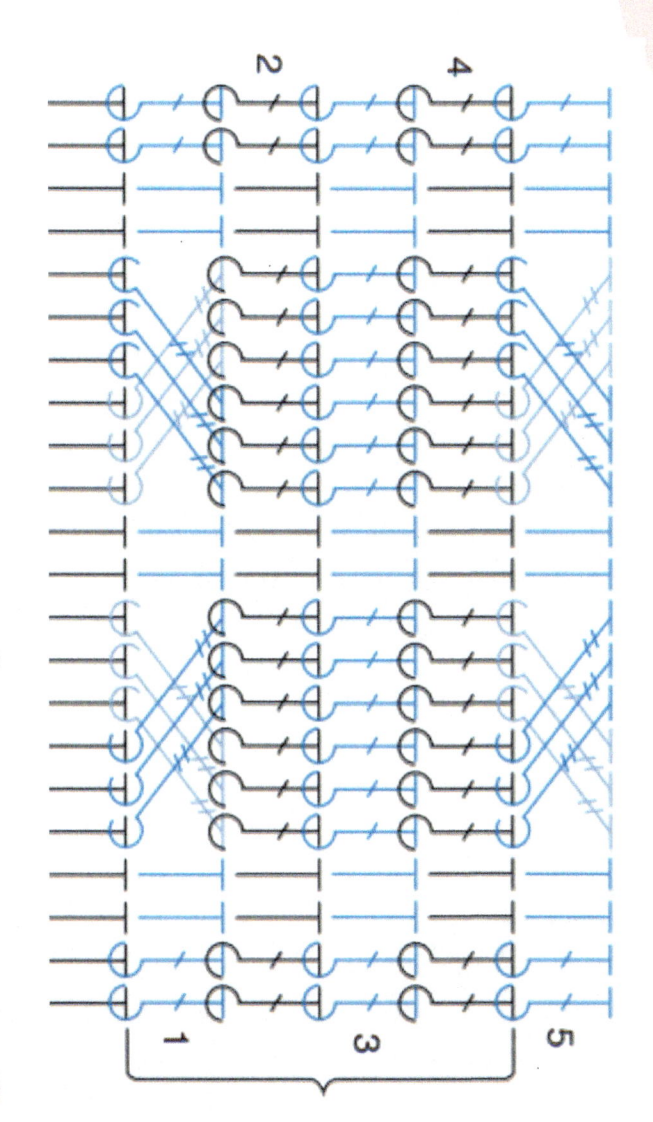

Shape Back:
- Next row: (RS). Sl st across the first 4 (5-7-8) sc. Ch 2. Hdc2tog. Pattern to the last 6 (7-9-10) sts. Hdc2tog. Turn. Leave remaining sts unworked. 36 (50-56-66) sts.
- Next row: Ch 2. Hdc2tog. Pattern to the last 2 sts. Hdc2tog. Turn.
- Repeat the last row 1 (4-6-7) more times. 32 (40-42-50) sts remain.
- Continue even in the pattern until the work from the first marker at neck ribbing measures 9 (12-15-18)" [23 (30.5-38-45.5) cm], ending on an RS row. Fasten off. Sew the neck and belly seam to the set of markers.

Back Edging:
- 1st rnd: (RS). Join yarn with sl st at seam. Ch 1. Work sc evenly around. Join with sl st to the first sc.
- 2nd rnd: Ch 1. 1 sc in each sc around. Join with sl st to the first sc.
- 3rd rnd: Ch 1. Working from left to right, instead of from right to left as usual, work 1 reverse sc in each sc around. Join with sl st to the first sc. Fasten off.

Leg Edging:
- 1st rnd: (RS). Join yarn with sl st at the leg opening. Ch 1. Work 16 (24-28-40) sc evenly around. Join with sl st to the first sc.
- 2nd to 6th rnds: Ch 1. 1 sc in each sc around. Join with sl st to the first sc.
- 7th rnd: Ch 1. Working from left to right, instead of from right to left as usual, work 1 reverse sc in each sc around. Join with sl st to the first sc. Fasten off.

CUTIE DOG SWEATER

Materials:
- RED HEART® With Love®:
- 1 skein each 1401 Pewter A, 1704 Bubblegum B, and 1502 Iced Aqua
- Susan Bates® Crochet Hook: 5.5mm [US I-9]
- Yarn needle

GAUGE:

- 12 sts = 4" (10 cm); 16 rows = 4" (10 cm). CHECK YOUR GAUGE. Use any size hook to obtain the gauge.
- Directions are for size Small. Changes for sizes Medium and Large are in parentheses.
- Finished Length: 12½ (13½, 14½)" [32 (34.5, 37) cm]
- Finished Chest: 14½ (19½, 24¼)" [37 (49.5, 61.5) cm]

Special Stitch
- Lsc (long single crochet) = Insert hook in bottom of indicated st 1 row below, yarn over and pull up a loop, yarn over and draw through both loops on hook.
- reverse sc (reverse single crochet) = Work single crochet in opposite direction from which you would usually work (left to right if you are right-handed and right to left if you are left-handed). This stitch is also known as crab stitch. It creates a rope-like twisted single crochet edging.
- sc2tog = [Insert hook in next stitch, yarn over and pull up a loop] twice, yarn over and draw through all 3 loops on hook.

Pattern Stitch
- Row 1 (wrong side): Ch 1, sc in first sc, *Lsc in next sc 1 row below, sc in next sc; repeat from * across, turn.
- Row 2: Ch 1, sc in each st across; change to next color in color sequence in last st, turn.

Color Sequence
- 2 rows with A, 2 rows with B, 2 rows with C

Notes
- To change color, work the last stitch of the old color to the last yarn over. Yarn over with the new color and draw through all loops on hook to complete the stitch. Proceed with the new color. Cut the old color or carry along the wrong side until next needed to minimize weaving in ends.
- Beginning at the end of Row 3 of Body, change to the next color in color sequence at the end of every other row.

SWEATER
- Neckband
- With A, ch 6.
- Row 1 (right side): Sc in 2nd ch from hook and in each ch across, turn—5 sts.
- Row 2: Ch 1, sc in back lp of each sc across, turn.
- Repeat the last row 27 (37, 47) times; change to B in last sc of last row.

BODY
- Row 1 (Right Side): Working in end of rows, ch 1, sc in each row across, turn—29 (39, 49) sc.
- Row 2: Ch 1, work 1 (2, 1) sc in first sc, *2 sc in next sc, sc in next sc; repeat from * across—43 (59, 73) sc.
- Row 3: Ch 1, sc in each sc across; change to B, turn.
- Rows 4 and 5: Work Rows 1 and 2 of pattern stitch.

DIVIDE FOR LEG OPENINGS
Right Underbody
- Row 1 (wrong side): Work Row 1 of pattern stitch in first 5 (7, 9) sts; leave remaining sts unworked, turn—5 (7, 9) sts.
- Rows 2–10 (14, 18): Work even in pattern stitch.
- Fasten off.

Center Back
- Row 1 (wrong side): With wrong side facing, skip next 3 (5, 7) sts of Row 5 of Body, join same color as Row 1 of Right Underbody with slip st in next st, beginning in same st as join, work Row 1 of pattern stitch in first 27 (35, 41) sts; leave remaining sts unworked, turn—27 (35, 41) sts.
- Rows 2–10 (14, 18): Work even in pattern stitch.
- Fasten off.

Left Underbody
- Row 1 (wrong side): With wrong side facing, skip next 3 (5, 7) sts of Row 5 of Body, join same color as Row 1 of Right Underbody with slip st in next st, beginning in same st as join, work Row 1 of pattern stitch in last 5 (7, 9) sts, turn—5 (7, 9) sts.
- Rows 2–10 (14, 18): Work even in pattern stitch.
- Do not fasten off.

BACK

- Row 11 (15, 19): Ch 1, sc in first sc, [Lsc in next sc 1 row below, sc in next sc] 2 (3, 4) times, ch 3 (5, 7), sc in next sc, [Lsc in next sc 1 row below, sc in next sc] 13 (17, 20) times, ch 3 (5, 7), repeat from * to * once, turn—37 (49, 59) sts and 6 (10, 14) ch.
- Row 12 (16, 20): Ch 1, sc in each st and ch across, turn—43 (59, 73) sts.
- Row 13 (17, 21): Work Row 1 of pattern stitch.
- Row 14 (18, 22): Ch 1, sc2tog, sc in each st across to last 2 sts, sc2tog, turn—41 (57, 71) sts.
- Rows 15–39 (19–43, 23–47): Repeat last 2 rows 12 times, then repeat last row once—15 (31, 45) sts.
- Fasten off.

LEG OPENING (work twice)

- Round 1 (right side): With right side facing, sc join A in any st at leg opening, sc evenly around; join with slip st in first sc.
- Round 2: Ch 1, sc in same st as join, *sc2tog, sc in next st; repeat from * around, adjusting at end of round as needed; join with slip st in first sc.
- Round 3: Ch 1, sc in each sc around; join with slip st in first sc.
- Rounds 4 and 5: Repeat Rounds 2 and 3.
- Round 6: Ch 1, reverse sc in each st around; join with slip st in first sc.
- Fasten off.

FINISHING

- With ends of rows held together, sew seam from Neckband to Row 14 (18, 22) of Back.

Edging
- Round 1 (right side): With right side of Back facing, sc join C (B, A) in seam, working in ends of rows and across last row, sc evenly around working 3 sc in each corner; join with slip st in first sc.
- Round 2: Ch 1, reverse sc in each st around; join with slip st in first sc.
- Fasten off.
- Weave in ends.

COZY CANINE

Materials:
- Caron® Cakes™ (7.1 oz/200 g; 383 yds/350 m)
- Sizes S M L XL balls Turkish Delight (17037) or Honey Berry (17044)
- 1 1 2 2 balls
- Sizes U.S. G/6 (4 mm) and U.S. 7 (4.5 mm) crochet hooks or size needed to obtain gauge.

GAUGE
- 14 sc and 15 rows = 4" [10 cm] with larger hook

INSTRUCTIONS
- The instructions are written for the smallest size. If changes are necessary for larger size(s), the instructions will be written thus ( ). Numbers for each size are shown in the same color throughout the pattern. When only one number is given in black, it applies to all sizes.

Neck Ribbing:
- With smaller hook, ch 17 (21-25-31) loosely.
    - 1st row: 1 sc in 2nd ch from hook. 1 sc in each ch to end of chain. Turn. 16 (20-24-30) sc.
    - 2nd row: Ch 1. Working in back loops only, work 1 sc in each st to end of row. Turn. Rep last row 30 (46-70-82) times more.

Body:
- Change to larger hook.
    - 1st row: (RS). Ch 1. Work 34 (50-74-86) sc across long edge of neck ribbing. Turn.
    - 2nd row: Ch 3 (counts as dc). *1 sc in next st. 1 dc in next st. Rep from * to last st. 1 sc in last st.
    - 3rd row: Ch 1. (1 sc. 1 dc) in first sc (inc made). *1 sc in next dc. 1 dc in next sc. Rep from * ending with (1 sc. 1 dc) in top of turning ch 3 (inc made). Turn.
    - 4th row: Ch 3 (counts as dc). 1 sc in first dc (inc made). *1 dc in next sc. 1 sc in next dc. Rep from * ending with (1 dc. 1 sc) in last sc (inc made). Turn.
    - Rep last 2 rows 1 (3-4-8) time(s) more. 42 (66-94-122) sts.

Shape Leg Opening: First Side:
- Next row: Ch 3 (counts as dc). Pat across next 5 (7-11-17) sts. Turn. Leave remaining sts unworked.
- Work 3 (3-5-7) rows even in pat over these 6 (8-12-18) sts. Fasten off.

Center Section:

- Next row: (RS). Skip next 4 (8-10-12) sts. Join yarn with sl st in next st. Ch 3 (counts as dc). Pat across next 21 (33-49-61) sts. Turn. Leave remaining sts unworked.
- Work 3 (3-5-7) rows even in pat over these 22 (34-50-62) sts. Fasten off.

Second Side:

- Next row: (RS). Skip next 4 (8-10-12) sts. Join yarn with sl st in next st. Ch 3 (counts as dc). Pat across next 5 (7-11-17) sts. Turn.
- Work 3 (3-5-7) rows even in pat over these 6 (8-12-18) sts. Do not fasten off.

Joining Row:

- (RS). Ch 3 (counts as dc). Pat across next 5 (7-11-17) sts of Second Side. Ch 4 (8-10-12) loosely. Pat across 22 (34-50-62) sts of Center Section. Ch 4 (8-10-12) loosely. Pat across 6 (8-12-18) sts of First Side. Turn.
- Next row: Ch 3 (counts as dc). Pat across next 5 (7-11-17) sts. Pat across next 4 (8-10-12) ch. Pat across next 22 (34-50-62) sts. Pat across next 4 (8-10-12) ch. Pat to end of row. Turn. 42 (66-94-122) sts.
- Work even in pat until work from Joining Row measures approx 5 (7-10½-12)" [12.5 (18-26.5-30.5) cm], ending on a WS row.

Shape Belly:
- Next row: Sl st in each of first 7 (11-15-19) sts. Ch 3 (counts as dc). Pat across next 29 (45-65-85) sts. Turn. Leave remaining sts unworked. 30 (46-66-86) sts.
- Next row: Ch 2 (does not count as st). hdc2tog over first 2 sts. Pat to last 2 sts. hdc2tog over last 2 sts. Turn.
- Rep last row 4 (5-8-12) times more. 20 (34-48-60) sts.
- Continue even in pat until work from 1st row after Neck Ribbing measures 10½ (16-21-24)" [26.5 (40.5-53.5-61) cm]. Fasten off.
- Sew seam from Neck Ribbing to Belly shaping.

Back Edging:
- (RS). Join yarn with sl st at seam. With larger hook, ch 1. Work 1 row sc evenly around Belly shaping and back edge, working 3 sc in corners. Join with sl st to first sc. Fasten off.

Leg Edging:
- (RS). Join yarn with sl st in any st of Leg Opening. With larger hook, ch 1. Work 1 row sc evenly around Leg Opening. Join with sl st to first sc. Fasten off.

Leg Bands (make 2):
- With smaller hook, ch 6 (6-8-8) loosely.
    - 1st row: 1 sc in 2nd ch from hook. 1 sc in each ch to end of chain. Turn. 5 (5-7-7) sc.
    - 2nd row: Ch 1. Working in back loops only, work 1 sc in each st to end of row. Turn. Rep last row until work (when slightly stretched) measures length to fit around Leg Edging. Fasten off.
    - Sew Leg Band seam. Sew side of Leg Band to Leg Edging.

Fold Neck Ribbing in half to WS and sew side edge loosely in position.

DAPPER PUP SWEATER

Materials:

Yarn:
- Caron® Simply Soft® (6 oz /170 g; 315 yds/288 m)
- Sizes S: 1 ball of Dark Sage (39707)
- Sizes M: 1 ball of Dark Sage (39707)
- Sizes L: 2 balls of Dark Sage (39707)
- Sizes XL: 2 balls of Dark Sage (39707)
- Crochet Hooks:
- U.S. G/6 (4 mm) and U.S. 7 (4.5 mm) or size needed to obtain gauge
- Additional Tools:
- Yarn needle

Gauge
- 14 double crochet (dc) and 8 rows = 4" [10 cm] with larger hook

Instructions

The instructions are written for the smallest size. Changes for larger sizes are written in parentheses. When only one number is given, it applies to all sizes.

Neck Ribbing

1. With smaller hook, ch 8.
   - 1st row: Ch 1, 1 single crochet (sc) in 2nd ch from hook, 1 sc in each ch to end of ch. Turn. (7 sc)
   - 2nd row: Ch 1, working in back loop only of each st, work 1 sc in each st to end of row. Turn.
   - Repeat 2nd row 30 (46-70-82) times more.

Body

1. Change to larger hook.
   - 1st row (RS): Ch 3 (counts as first dc), work a further 33 (49-73-85) dc across long edge of neck ribbing. (34 (50-74-86) dc). Turn.
   - 2nd row: Ch 3, 1 dc in first dc (increase (inc) made), 1 dc in each dc to last dc, 2 dc in last dc (inc made). Turn.
   - Repeat 2nd row 2 (6-10-16) times more. (40 (64-96-120) dc)

Shape Leg Opening: First Side
1. Next row: Ch 3 (counts as dc), 1 dc in each of next 4 (7-11-15) dc. (5 (8-12-16) dc). Turn. Leave remaining stitches (sts) unworked.
2. Next row: Ch 3 (counts as dc), 1 dc in each dc to end of row. Turn.
3. Repeat last row 1 (3-5-5) time(s) more. Fasten off.

Center Section
1. Next row: With RS facing, skip next 4 (7-9-12) dc, join yarn with sl st in next dc. Ch 3 (counts as dc), 1 dc in each of next 21 (33-53-63) dc. (22 (34-54-64) dc). Turn. Leave remaining stitches unworked.
2. Next row: Ch 3 (counts as dc), 1 dc in each dc to end of row. Turn.
3. Repeat last row 1 (3-5-5) time(s) more. Fasten off.

Second Side
1. Next row: With RS facing, skip next 4 (7-9-12) unworked dc, join yarn with sl st in next dc. Ch 3 (counts as dc), 1 dc in each of next 4 (7-11-15) dc. (5 (8-12-16) dc). Turn.
2. Next row: Ch 3 (counts as dc), 1 dc in each dc to end of row. Turn.
3. Repeat last row 1 (3-5-5) time(s) more.

Joining Row
1. Next row: Ch 3 (counts as dc), 1 dc in each dc across Second Side, ch 4 (7-9-12) loosely, 1 dc in each dc across Center Section, ch 4 (7-9-12) loosely, 1 dc in each dc across First Side. Turn.
2. Next row: Ch 3 (counts as dc), 1 dc in each of next 4 (7-9-12) dc, 1 dc in each of next 4 (7-9-12) ch, 1 dc in each of next 22 (34-54-64) dc, 1 dc in each of next 4 (7-9-12) ch, 1 dc in each of next 5 (8-10-13) dc. (40 (64-96-120) dc). Turn.
3. Next row: Ch 3 (counts as dc), 1 dc in each dc to end of row. Turn.
4. Repeat last row until work from Joining Row measures approx 4½ (7-10½-11½)" [11.5 (18-26.5-29) cm], ending with RS facing for next row.

Shape Belly

1. Next row: Sl st in each of first 7 (10-15-19) dc, ch 3 (counts as dc), 1 dc in each of next 27 (45-67-83) dc. Turn. Leave remaining stitches unworked. (28 (46-68-84) dc)
2. Next row: Ch 3 (counts as dc), (yarn over hook (yoh) and draw up a loop in next st, yoh and draw through 2 loops on hook) twice, yoh and draw through all loops on hook - dc2tog made, 1 dc in each dc to last 3 dc, dc2tog, 1 dc in last dc. Turn.
3. Repeat last row 3 (6-9-11) times more. (20 (32-48-60) dc)
4. Continue even until work from 1st row after Neck Ribbing measures 10½ (16-22-25)" [26.5 (40.5-56-63.5) cm]. Fasten off. Sew seam from Neck Ribbing to Belly shaping.

Back Edging

1. With RS facing and larger hook, join yarn with sl st at seam. Ch 1.
   - Work 1 row sc evenly around Belly shaping and back edge, working 3 sc in corners.
   - Join with sl st to first sc. Fasten off.

Leg Edging

1. With RS facing and larger hook, join yarn with sl st in any st of Leg Opening. Ch 1.
   - Work 1 row sc evenly around Leg Opening.
   - Join with sl st to first sc. Fasten off.

Leg Bands
1. With smaller hook, ch 6.
    - 1st row: 1 sc in 2nd ch from hook, 1 sc in each ch to end of ch. Turn. (5 sc)
    - 2nd row: Ch 1, working in back loop only of each st, work 1 sc in each st to end of row. Turn.
    - Repeat last row until work from beginning measures 5 (6-8-9½)" [12.5 (15-20.5-24) cm]. Fasten off.
    - Sew Leg Band seam.
    - Sew Leg Band to Leg Edging.

DEVIL DOG

Materials:
- RED HEART® SuperSaver™
- 1 skein of 319 Cherry Red (A)
- 1 skein of 312 Black (B)
- Crochet Hook: 5.5mm [US I-9]

Gauge:
12 stitches = 4". Check your gauge and adjust the hook size as needed to obtain the specified gauge.

Additional Tools:
- Yarn needle
- One button (7/8" diameter)
- Two 1" D-rings
- 2½" square of cardboard

Finished Measurements
- Chest: 16-19 (20-25, 26-32)"
- Length: 10 (14, 17)"

Note: Sweater is worked from the neck down.

Collar

1. With B, ch 38 (50, 62).
    - Row 1 (RS): Dc in 4th ch from hook and in each ch across, turn – 36 (48, 60) dc.
    - Row 2: Ch 3 (counts as dc), dc in each across. Fasten off.

Body

1. Row 1: With right side facing, skip first 3 (5, 7) sts, join A in next st, ch 3, dc in next 29 (37, 45) dc, turn, leaving last 3 (5, 7) sts unworked – 30 (38, 46) dc.
2. Row 2: Ch 3, dc in first st, dc in next and each st to within last st, 2 dc in last st, turn – 32 (40, 48) sts.
3. Row 3: Ch 3, dc in each st across, turn.
4. Rows 4-16 (22, 28): Repeat Rows 2-3 for 7 (10, 13) times more – 46 (60, 74) sts.
5. Fasten off.

Edging

1. Row 1: With right side facing, join B with sc at upper Body next to Collar, work 23 (33, 48) sc along side to corner, work 3 sc in corner, work 44 (58, 72) sc along lower edge, work 3 sc in corner, work 24 (34, 39) sc along side to upper Body, ending at lower Collar.
2. Row 2: Ch 1, work backwards sc in each st around. Fasten off.

Pitchfork

- Center:
    - With B, ch 13 (15, 17).
    - (Slip st, ch 5, slip st, ch 3, slip st) in 3rd ch from hook, slip st in each ch to end.
    - Fasten off.
- Side Spokes:
    - With B, ch 10 (12, 14).
    - Slip st in 3rd ch from hook, slip st in each ch across, ch 3, slip st in last ch.
    - Fasten off.

Finishing
1. Following the photo, sew the Pitchfork to the back.
2. Sew the button to the end of the collar. Button slips between sts to close.

Horned Headpiece

Band
1. With B, ch 16 (18, 20).
    - Row 1: Sc in 2nd ch from hook and in each ch across, turn – 15 (17, 19) sc.
    - Rows 2-5: Ch 1, sc in each st across, turn. Fasten off.

Ties
- With B, place slip knot on hook, working in edges of rows, pull slip knot through first st, [pull yarn through next st] 4 times, yo, pull yarn through all 5 loops on hook.
    - Ch 35 (40, 45).
    - Slip st in 2nd ch from hook and in ch across. Fasten off.
- Repeat at opposite end for second Tie.

Horns (Make 2)
- With A, ch 2.
    - Round 1: Work 3 sc in 2nd ch from hook – 3 sc.
    - Round 2: Work 2 sc in each sc around – 6 sc.
    - Round 3: Sc in each sc around – 6 sc.
    - Round 4: [Sc in next sc, 2 sc in next sc] 3 times – 9 sc.
    - Round 5: Sc in each sc around – 9 sc.
    - Round 6: [Sc in next 2 sc, 2 sc in next sc] 3 times – 12 sc.
    - Rounds 7-8 (9): Sc in each sc around. On the last round, slip st to first st to join.
    - Fasten off.
- Stuff each horn with a small amount of A. Sew horns to Band.

Dear Reader,

Thank you so much for choosing "Crochet for Dog: A collection of adorable crochet sweaters for your pets"

I'm absolutely thrilled that you've picked up my book. I put a lot of love and effort into creating it, and I truly hope you enjoy every page. Inside, you'll find a variety of crochet patterns for adorable sweaters for your furry friends. The patterns are designed to be fun and easy to follow, whether you're a beginner or have been crocheting for years. Plus, they can all be made with worsted weight yarn. I hope you find lots of patterns that you'll love to make. Happy crocheting, and I can't wait to see what you create!

Warmest wishes,

Printed in Great Britain
by Amazon